T0065697

WHAT SHALL WE DO?

A Guide For New Believers

RICK CUMMINS

WESTBOW
PRESS®
A DIVISION OF THOMAS NELSON
& ZONDERVAN

WestBow Press books may be ordered through booksellers or by contacting:

WestBow Press
A Division of Thomas Nelson & Zondervan
1663 Liberty Drive
Bloomington, IN 47403
www.westbowpress.com
844-714-3454

ISBN: 978-1-6642-7901-8 (sc)
ISBN: 978-1-6642-7902-5 (hc)
ISBN: 978-1-6642-7900-1 (e)

Library of Congress Control Number: 2022917834

Print information available on the last page.

WestBow Press rev. date: 9/26/2022

INTRODUCTION

Since you are reading this book, it likely means you have just made the most important decision of your life; you have just asked Jesus to be the Lord and Savior of your life. The first thing I would like to say is welcome to the family. For the last two thousand years or so, many people all over the world have been making this decision, just like you have today, and you all have one thing in common. You have questions.

You may be asking several right now. One may be, "What did I just do?" or maybe, "What does this mean?"

Really, it all comes down to one important question that is asked every time the gospel is preached and accepted. It is the same question that was asked on the very first day that the Church sprang into existence.

In the book of Acts, it says, "When the people heard this, they were cut to the heart and said to Peter and the other apostles, 'Brothers, what shall we do?'" (Acts 2:37 New International Version).

Peter simply replied, "Repent and be baptized, every one of you, in the name of Jesus Christ for the forgiveness of your sins. And you will receive the gift of the Holy Spirit" (Acts 2:38 NIV).

Well, that seems easy enough, right? The author of Acts goes on to say, "With many other words, he warned them; and he pleaded with them, 'Save yourselves from this corrupt generation.' Those who accepted his message were baptized" (Acts 2:40 NIV).

This verse is important because there is no simple answer to the question "what shall we do?" In the book of Acts, the writer basically says, I want to encourage you today by saying it's OK if you don't have all the answers. It's OK if you have questions. It's OK if you have doubts. It's OK if you don't really know what to do. After this, the people who accepted the message of the gospel walked a long road of discipleship. For the rest of their lives, they diligently learned what it meant to make the same decision you made today. No one figures it out instantly. Paul writes a letter to the Philippian Church and says, "Therefore, my dear friends, as you have always obeyed—not only in my presence but now much more in my absence—continue to work out your salvation with fear and trembling" (Philippians 2:12 NIV).

The truth is that this moment now is the beginning of a lifelong journey that you will have with Jesus and those around you as you work out your salvation. If you read the rest of the book of Acts, you will see all the amazing things all the believers did—how they raised the dead, healed the sick, evangelized the world, fed the hungry, clothed the needy, and rescued sinners from the clutches of hell. However, there is no list of rules or dos and don'ts. There is no checklist that we can follow to make sure we get it all right. The only thing we really have is the model of those who came before us and the life of Jesus as He essentially said, "I am the way—basically, follow me, and do what I do." This is the true nature of growth and discipleship.

As you go through this book, I want to take you through some essential fundamentals in the Bible about who Jesus is, who we are, and what this thing is that we call church. Before you close the book and stop reading in fear of boredom, I promise this will not be a deep theological book not for the faint of heart. These will be simple, real, everyday truths that will help you understand what it means to be a Christian.

PART 1

ONE

THE FAMILY

◆◆◆◆◆◆◆

The Church Is Not an Organization; It Is a Family

Growing up in the church, I have seen a lot of wonderful and terrifying things in and around it. Some of my favorite moments were during revival meetings, which often went on all week. We had music, and some evangelist would come in and preach his heart out. He told of the wonders of God and explained that God wanted to heal and deliver us.

In these meetings, I saw so many miraculous wonders from God. During one service, a lady who had one leg that was three inches shorter than the other one was met by the healing evangelist. He sat her in a chair and had her hold out her legs so everyone could see how irregular they were. At that moment, he prayed to God, and before my eyes I saw her left leg grow until it met the length of the other leg.

As a young child, I thought, *Wow! This is it! This is the reason why the church exists!* In my mind, it couldn't get better than this. But then the revival ended, the evangelist went home, and there we were, back into everyday life.

As I got older, after seeing a few more evangelistic revival meetings, I learned that this evangelist had the best job in the world. He went from place to place doing wonderful things, and then after he finished and the message went out he left town, and we rarely saw him again. He didn't have to sit by the bedside of the woman dying of cancer when God didn't perform the miracle. He didn't have to visit the man who can't work anymore because of injury and was denied disability. This evangelist didn't have to walk and guide people through the understanding that they decided to follow Jesus, but they didn't feel any different. He got to come into town, add a bunch of numbers to his tally card of healing and salvation, and then move on to the next place.

One thing I learned most from these experiences was that Jesus is not trying to build an organization. Jesus is not trying to build a ministry or draw a crowd, and He did not come to the world and die on a cross to make a leg grow longer. Now don't get me wrong. Jesus loves to heal us, to make our lives better, and He loves to perform miracles. What I am saying is this is not why He came; it was merely something He did while he was here. Jesus came for one reason and one reason only: to die for your sins so that you could be set free and become part of the family of God. He came so that your life, when put in His story, can show His glory. Jesus died so you could be part of God's family. This was the greatest revelation in my life, even though it seems so simple. The kingdom of God, the church, and all its people are part of a family. We can learn many things about God and His kingdom by taking a deeper dive into this idea of family.

No matter what your family structure looked like growing up, many things in every family are the same. I want to be clear: I believe there is a biblical way the family should function, but I am not trying to tell you what your family should look like. I am simply using the family to show what the church is supposed to look like, because that's what Jesus did.

So if the church is supposed to be a family, what does that mean? The first obvious thing about family is that you are born into it. The same is true of God's family. I am sure most of us growing up have heard someone at some time use the term *born again*. This term did not come from human theologians trying to describe an eternal truth; this term came straight from the mouth of Jesus. In the gospel of John, Jesus met with one of the religious leaders named Nicodemus late at night. This leader was asking Jesus about the kingdom of God. Jesus said to him, "Truly, truly, I say to you, unless one is born again, he cannot see the kingdom of God" (John 3:3 NIV).

This is a big statement for Jesus to make, and many of us may have the same question that Nicodemus had: How can I do this? But Jesus is not talking about physical birth. Flesh gives birth to flesh, but the Spirit gives birth to Spirit. With this, we understand that when we decide to follow Jesus, the Spirit of God comes inside us and gives birth to a new Spirit the same way the Spirit came on to Mary, the mother of Jesus, and gave birth to Jesus, the Christ. Jesus was born of the Spirit of God, and now so are you.

Another reference that Paul uses to talk about entering the family of God is in a letter to the church in Ephesus. He writes, "God decided in advance to adopt us into His own family by bringing us to Himself through Jesus Christ. This is what He wanted to do, and it gave Him great delight" (Ephesians 1:5). Here we have the idea of adoption, but it is not just an afterthought. God decided in advance that He wanted you, and He chose you to be part of His family. I love the last part of this verse that says it gave Him great delight. This is one of the most powerful pieces of the kingdom; it is something we all need to understand from the beginning: we are children of God.

Another distinction of the family that we can look at to understand the kingdom is that in a family, we all serve at times, and we are all served at times. I still remember a conversation I had with my dad as a child at the dinner table. I had finished my plate, and the food was so delicious, I wanted more.

I looked at my dad and said, "Dad, can you get me some more?"

Although at the time I did not like his answer, now that I am a dad I find myself saying the same thing to my kids. He looked at me and said, "Are your legs broke? Go get it yourself."

Now that you have all taken a moment to let that sink in, let me clarify that my dad was the most loving father I could have ever asked for. He would do anything for me, and his only dream in life was for us boys (my brother and me) to be successful in life. But at this moment, he was trying to teach me a lesson: at some point in a family, you must do your part to serve the house.

After this, my parents gave us chores; we had to help. We did the dishes, mowed the grass, cleaned our rooms, and took out the trash. The older we got, the longer our chore list got. It wasn't because my parents could not do everything themselves; they'd done it all without my help when I was a baby. But now they were allowing me to be part of the family. If you do not serve the house, you are probably a guest in the house, but if you are a member of the family, as you mature, you serve.

John, in his gospel narrative, says, "But to all who did receive him, who believed in his name, he gave the right to become children of God" (John 1:12). The word that stands out to me in this verse is *right*. John said that when we receive Jesus and believe in Him, He gives us the right to become children of God. This says to me that some people who have received and believed did not become members of the family of God. This verse is saying that when we become members of God's family, we not only get access to all His blessings but also the burden of His commandments.

Jesus had three commands in the New Testament: to "love God with all your heart, soul, and mind" (Mark 12:30); "Love your neighbor as yourself" (Mark 12:31); and "Go into all the world and preach the gospel, making disciples of all people and baptizing them" (Matthew 28:19–20).

I want to be clear. I am not saying you must serve to be saved. You are saved by faith alone. It is not believe and serve and you will be saved. However, I do believe

Jesus puts a strong emphasis on the fact that although we are justified by faith alone, we must still work out our salvation and grow. In my house, I did not serve because I was a slave; I served because I was a son.

The last things about the family that I want to mention are love and acceptance, which will help us better understand the church. When my brother and I were young, we fought all the time. We argued, yelled, punched each other, and wrestled around, but we were still brothers at the end of the day. No matter how mad we got, no matter how much our feelings got hurt, we still loved each other. We had wonderful moments that I will cherish, and we had downright dirty moments where I am amazed we didn't kill each other.

But at some point, no matter how hard it is, no matter how much time has passed, no matter what they did to wrong you, they are family.

This is much how it should be with the church. Like family, we often have a weakness for each other. We often overlook each other's faults, understand the worst, and can usually find the best. When we become part of God's family, we have love and acceptance for

His church, although no church is perfect, and they make mistakes, they may offend or hurt and abuse. Still, at the end of the day, we love the church, because it is a family. If God has not put a love for the church that can see the good and overlook fault, then I would question if you have truly been born into the family of God.

I want to add something to the end of this. I know some people out there have been truly hurt by a church member, clergy, or a pastor, and what they did to you was horrible. It may be something that created an irreparable separation from those people. I do not want in any way to say that what you're feeling isn't real or relevant. Rather, I want to say those people who hurt you do not represent the entire church or the family of God. I want to encourage you to allow God to heal that wound by allowing you to see the good in who He is. People will always disappoint you, but God is always faithful, and His love will never fail you.

Now that we have talked about the church and what it is, I want us to discover why the church exists. The church does not exist to draw big crowds, although it can do that. The church does not exist to make money or put on conferences or events. The church exists to give you a place to belong, to be a safe place for each one of us when we are joined in to the family of God to grow and mature. The church exists for each one of us to find our passion and calling. The church exists to give a place of empowerment to each one of us as we give our lives to Jesus. The church exists to give you identity in Christ. Finally, the church exists as a place for us to show grace, love, and acceptance to all who are in need or cast out.

TWO

WHO AM I? (IDENTITY)

--------- ✦ ✦ ✦✦✦ ✦ ✦ ---------

If the church exists to give us identity in Christ, that brings us to ask a new question: Who am I? This is a question that every single one of us has asked ourselves a few times in our lives. Not just who am I, but who do I want to be? Isn't that the fundamental question we ask as children? What do I want to be when I grow up? This question plagues us as humans. Essentially, we are asking much deeper questions that most of us probably don't even realize we are asking. Still, the questions come out in how we act, what we do, where we go, and how we live. Those deeper questions that we are asking are am I valuable? Do I have a purpose? Does my life have meaning? And what if I don't fit what society says I should be?

The only way to answer these questions is to look at the very beginning. Not the very beginning of me or you but the very beginning of it all. As Christians, we have a unique worldview that says there is one God and that God created everything. That may sound simple in itself, but there is more. There are many creation myths, essentially origin stories. And the one thing they all have in common is that god or the gods created man to serve them. The gods of all religions made man, and man was destined to serve at the will of the gods. Mankind was insignificant. We didn't really matter. We were dispensable. But with the one true God, the God of biblical creation, the God who sent Jesus to the earth, the eternal God of the universe, God did not create us to serve Him or be a slave to His will. No. God created us with the glory of His essence; God created us in His image.

Let's look at this together.

> Then God said, "Let us make mankind
> in our image, in our likeness, so that they
> may rule over the fish in the sea and the
> birds in the sky, over the livestock and
> all the wild animals, and over all the

creatures that move along the ground." So God created mankind in his own image, in the image of God he created them; male and female he created them. God blessed them and said to them, "Be fruitful and increase in number; fill the earth and subdue it. Rule over the fish in the sea and the birds in the sky and over every living creature that moves on the ground." (Gen 1:26–28 NIV)

We can pull out some of the most important things about our identity in this verse. The first is that God created us in His image. Well, what is so important about that? This means we have intrinsic value. You are valuable. You are not valuable because you accomplished great things because you had not accomplished anything at the moment of creation. You are not valuable because of your talent or your potential. You are not valuable because of what you have achieved or because of what you will achieve. You are not valuable because you are beautiful. You are simply valuable because you were made in the image, the very likeness, of God.

The second thing we see in this verse is that we were not created to serve or to be a slave to the will of a tyrant god, but we were made to rule. This idea is revolutionary in the eyes of religion, and I believe this is the reason people have issues with abandonment, identity, self-esteem, and self-worth. We still believe we were made and put on this earth to serve. Now don't get me wrong—we are not God or tiny versions of Him. We are merely an image or a likeness of God. Imagine taking a family picture and then setting it on the shelf for everyone to see. When you look at the picture, you will see the image of you, maybe your husband or wife, maybe your kids or whomever else may be in that portrait. We will all look at that picture and recognize who is there, but we will all clearly understand that the image there is not actually you. It is simply your image. In this same way, we are made in the image of God.

The idea that God did not create us to serve but to rule is an important element of understanding your identity. When we understand this, we can move past the mind-set of obligated service to God. We can move into a relationship with God where he designed us to go rule with his image and authority.

The next thing God said in this origin story was that after He created mankind in His image, He blessed them. God has already blessed you. Ephesians 1:3 says it like this: "Praise be to the God and Father of our Lord Jesus Christ, who has blessed us in the heavenly realms with every spiritual blessing in Christ" (NIV).

This is saying that no matter how much you pray for it, God cannot bless you any more than He already has because you have been blessed from the beginning. Then it was amplified with Christ. When we make Christ our head and give Him authority over our lives, we have every spiritual blessing.

Finally, we see a purpose in it all. It's like when the sun starts shining on a foggy day, we see a full picture of what is going on around us.

I want you to understand that this is before sin, before Adam and Eve ate the fruit, this account of you and me and mankind is at the beginning. This tells us this is the original design. When sin entered our hearts and created separation from God and death for mankind, it broke the design that God had intended for us. God did not intend for us to be a slave to sin.

God intended us to rule with His image and spread His image throughout the world. However, with sin, the cloud of death ruled instead. That was why Jesus came: to break the chains of death that were holding us back from being who God created us to be. Jesus came so we could return to the plan, to being the representation of His image and His glory throughout the world. When we finally realize who we are, that we are made by God, in His image, no mistakes, no mess-ups, but He made you exactly the way He wanted you, you will begin to understand that you have value and are glorious.

Our world today is not short of identity issues. Over the years our corrupted society and gender roles have made it impossible for young men and women to see the value in themselves as God created them. And the truth is, you do not need to change yourself to fit in to God's identity for you. He made you, He understands you, and He loves you, and You reflect His glory when you stand up tall, just the way He made you. In Jesus alone, you will find your identity. Outside of Christ, we are covered in the cloud of death. We cannot outshine God's glory; we cannot see the value in what He has made. When we allow Jesus to be Lord of our lives, He is the light that breaks through the darkness of our insecurity. He shines His light into our hearts so that the world, through us, can see His glory. Then and only then will you understand your true value and identity.

At the end of the day, never forget these words. Say them to yourself every time you doubt, every time you feel like you are not good enough, every time you feel pushed down. "I am a child of God. That is who I am. Nothing can change that because I was born of His Spirit. I was made in His likeness to bear His image and show His glory throughout the world."

If we are going to bear the image of God, if we are going to be the ambassadors of God, if we are to be the example and representation of God to the world, we should know who He is. This idea of knowing God has been on the minds of humankind from the beginning. That is the intrinsic nature of religion itself, finding a way to God—to know Him, to understand Him. So if we are going to spread the image of God across the world, we must ask the question. Who is God?

THREE

WHO IS GOD? (SOVEREIGNTY)

I decided to do a test yesterday to see what was out there, and I Googled my question: Who is God? I was amazed at all the things I saw. There were sites talking about all kinds of gods and sites talking about the God of the Bible, but when I opened them up, they were just as odd as all the rest. Then it dawned on me, and it was not a new revelation, just something the Lord brought to the front of my mind. This is the nature of religion.

The basic principle of religion is teaching humankind how to get to god or find god. So, naturally, all these sites that I opened were trying to do just that. They were trying to rationalize, find, understand, humanize, or prove the existence of God, when, in fact, the Bible says that nature itself points to the glory of God: "The heavens declare the glory of God; the skies proclaim the work of his hands" (Psalm 19:1 NIV).

The one thing that makes Christianity different from all the other religions of the world is simple. The first we talked about in the previous section: you were not created to serve but to rule and spread the image and glory of God across the world. The second is just as revolutionary. God did not leave us to find our way to Him; rather, He sent His one and only begotten Son to earth to show us the way.

Jesus says it like this: "Jesus answered, 'I am the way and the truth and the life. No one comes to the Father except through me'" (John 14:6 NIV).

So many people look at this verse and think Christianity is narrow-minded or exclusive. But this verse is not exclusive at all. It is, in truth, the opposite. This verse shows God's love and His heart to all of us. Jesus did not just leave us alone to figure out how to get to God or heaven on our own. Rather, He came down from heaven and told us as plainly as He could, as loud as He could,

"Hey! If you are looking for God, you want to hear this. I will tell you exactly how to get there. You must come through me. I am the way." This verse was in response to his disciples asking the same question everyone else on earth was asking: How will we know the way?

Jesus is quite deliberate when He says this as well. He does not want to leave anything to chance. He knows that we, on our own, could never be good enough to find God or even know God. So He showed us the way. In the same way, He also told us how to know and see God. He said this in the gospel of John: "Jesus answered: 'Don't you know me, Philip, even after I have been among you such a long time? Anyone who has seen me has seen the Father. How can you say, "Show us the Father"?'" (John 14:9 NIV).

Unlike any other religion in the world, God did not want us to have to navigate through mystery and cryptic text to try to unravel the mystery of who He is. He sent Jesus to live in human flesh to show us who He is and how to find Him. All we need to do is look to Jesus and follow Him.

I would like to encourage you to take some time to meditate on this and pray for understanding. Once we understand that we do not have to work to get to God, but rather He did all the work and came to us, we can move into the question of who He is. It is one thing to know how to find God; it is another to know who He is. When the apostle Paul went to Athens to preach the gospel, he found a religious culture. They worshiped many gods and set up shrines and images of worship for each of them.

However, one shrine was set up that Paul described as the unknown god: "For as I walked around and looked carefully at your objects of worship, I even found an altar with this inscription: to an unknown god. So you are ignorant of the very thing you worship— and this is what I am going to proclaim to you" (Acts 17:23 NIV).

Paul shares with them the very nature of who God is, and some asked Paul to come and tell them more about this. See, when we get a glimpse of who God is, it changes us. We have to know more, to see more; it creates desire, passion, and a drive to share what you have seen in the world. This is what happens when you truly see God for who He is. Let's dive into this question.

Who Is God?

In the Bible, especially the Old Testament, names were meaningful. They carried identity and special understanding. In some sense, you were almost described by your name. For example, if you grew up in church, you would remember a story about a man named Jacob. You can find this story in Genesis 27. Jacob was the son of Isaac, the son of Abraham, who God had called out of the land he lived in and into the Promised Land. Abraham was the one God promised to make into a great nation, and from him came the nation of Israel.

So here we have Abraham's grandson Jacob. The most famous act that Jacob is known for is stealing his brother's birthright. His brother was a great hunter, and he was told to go out hunting and bring back some food for his old blind father. As soon as he walked out the door, Jacob and his mother devised a plan to dress Jacob up in goatskin and put it all over his arms, as his brother was hairy and he was not. They did this to deceive his father so Jacob could steal the blessing that was not meant for him from his father. I am telling you this story to illustrate a point. The name Jacob literally means deceiver. Jacob became the very person his name portrayed him to be.

This is the reason why, when Jacob was in the wilderness many years later, afraid to confront his brother, God appeared and wrestled with him. At the end of It, Jacob demanded of God that He bless him. When God blessed him and made a covenant with him, God did something that we often see in scripture. He changed his name from Jacob, meaning deceiver, to Israel, meaning the one who struggles with God.

If the scriptures put this kind of meaning on names, where the name you are given is something that identifies and defines you, then naturally, the best place to start looking at the nature of God would be to look at the names of God.

In the Old Testament, there are many names for God. This is not saying the names of the religions in the world are all referring to the same god. If you look at each religion and you look at what it claims and what it offers you in the end, they are all different, and all are different from the one true God. However, the names of God come from what people in the scriptures saw of His divine nature. There were a few names that God revealed of Himself, and there were many that people used to describe His wonder.

I would like to look at these names of God from the Old Testament and see if they will bring some illumination to this question of "who is God?" And since God never changes, who He was then is the same as who He is today.

We will look at many names that start with the root word *el*. This is a word in Hebrew that just means God, and it is usually followed by a second word to describe the character of God that this name reveals.

El Shaddai (Lord God Almighty)

The word Shaddai, without going into too much of the word's etymology, denotes a God who freely gives nourishment and blessing to His people. Simply put, it means God sustains us; thus, He is the Lord God Almighty. This name for God was first used in the

Old Testament when God revealed Himself to Abram and said, "I am the Almighty God" (see Genesis 17:1).

El Elyon (the Most-High God)

The word *Elyon* is a Hebrew word that is literally translated as most high. This word expresses God's ultimate sovereignty and majesty. God is all supreme and has power and control over everything. We see this name used a lot in the psalms, and I love how King David uses it when he is hiding from Saul in a cave. He writes: "I will cry out to God Most High, to God who performs all things for me" (Psalm 57:2 New King James Version).

This is a moment we see a man who understands the sovereignty of God even in a moment where he was likely to die. David had been anointed king, but Saul still held the throne. Saul was seeking to kill David any chance he could get. Then in this beautiful moment, David cries out to the Most-High God.

Adonai (Lord, Master)

The word *Adonai* is used 434 times in the Old Testament. This name for God is often used as a substitute for the name Yahweh, most likely for the Hebrew people to avoid the improper use of God's name (see Exodus 20:7). Adonai is both plural and possessive in the Hebrew language. This is one of the great mysteries of God as God says of Himself that there is one God, yet we have three distinct persons that He reveals Himself in all through the scriptures. He is God the Father, He is also Jesus, who is God, and He is the Holy Spirit, who is also God. And they are one. Adonai.

My purpose here is not to explain God's complexities but to describe the nature of God. The thing that we need to understand is that God is one, yet He is all three. He is God the Father, God the Son (Jesus), and God the Holy Spirit.

One scripture in the New Testament where you can see all three at work in the same moment is at the time Jesus was baptized. "As soon as Jesus was baptized, he went up out of the water. At that moment, heaven was opened, and he saw the Spirit of God descending like a dove and alighting on him. And a voice from heaven said, 'This is my Son, whom I love; with him I am well pleased'" (Matthew 3:16–17 NIV).

This is a beautiful moment in scripture where we see God. Jesus was fully God in human flesh, and He was baptized. The Holy Spirit descended and rested on Him. Then the Father spoke. This, to me, is one of the clearest pictures of God in the scriptures.

Yahweh (Lord, Jehovah)

Now that we talked about the substitute for the name Yahweh, let's look at the name itself. Yahweh is the most used name for God in the scriptures. It was used 6,519 times. This name was so special and held such reverence in the original Hebrew spelling they did not use any vowels. They said it in almost a whisper, YHWH, because the name was too holy to even voice.

The name Yahweh was first used in Genesis 2 when God was described as resting after the world was made. However, He revealed Himself using this name for the first time in Exodus 3, when God spoke to Moses in the burning bush. Why was this name so holy? Because it denotes the omnipotence of God. That simply means this name shows and describes a God who is all-powerful and unmatched. He is revealed as the God who created and formed the universe. It was the name given when God said to Moses, "I am." They were also the same words Jesus said when He was arrested that caused everyone to fall flat on their backs just at the words. This name carried ultimate power.

El Olam (the Everlasting God)

I love this name for God because the word Olam literally means forever. When you join this word with the root word el, you get a word that just simply means Eternal God. And this is true of Him. He was before time, He will be after time, He was not created, and He cannot be uncreated. He just is. He is an Everlasting God. This name was first used in Genesis 21:33.

Qanna (Jealous)

This is a really important name for God because it is often used in the sense of a husband's jealous love for his wife. God is described as the Husband to Israel, just as Jesus is described as the Bridegroom of the Church. This name denotes God's desire to have us all to Himself. He does not want to share us with the lustful and selfish desires of this earth. God desires our full devotion and 100 percent of our love and affection. We see this when He gives the ten commandments and says, "You shall not bow down to them or worship them; for I, the Lord your God, am a jealous God, punishing the children for the sin of the parents to the third and fourth generation of those who hate me" (Exodus 20:5 NIV).

In Exodus, God also says this of Himself when the Israelites constantly looked to the gods of the nations around them and worshiped them. "For thou shalt worship no other god: for the Lord, whose name is Jealous, is a jealous God" (Exodus 34:14 King James Version).

Elohim (God)

Elohim is the name of God used in (Genesis 1:1) that says, in the beginning, God created. This word for God is often used around the idea of creation.

It denotes a God who operates with extraordinary control over human affairs. The name Elohim is used two thousand times in the scriptures and translated into words like creator or judge. At the end of the day, God created everything and is in control of everything.

There are many more names in the scriptures that describe the nature of God, but the names that we talked about here we'll sum up by meaning in a list. We have God, and His names are Almighty, Most High, Lord, Master, All-Powerful, Everlasting, Jealous, and Creator. The most wonderful thing about the magnificence of the list of names of God is one simple truth. He loved you so much that He sent His only begotten Son so that whosoever believes in Him will not perish but have everlasting life (see John 3:16). This is probably the most famous verse in the Bible because of how unbelievable it is for an all-powerful God to die for us.

In the New Testament, when we talk about names for God, I see many places that tell us that Jesus is the name above every other name. Still, I think one name gives a beautiful picture of who God is as we relate to Him under the new covenant of Jesus's sacrifice for us, and that is Abba. This word literally means daddy. "The Spirit you received does not make you slaves, so that you live in fear again; rather, the Spirit you received brought about your adoption to Sonship. And by him we cry, 'Abba, Father'" (Romans 8:15 NIV).

God is the perfect Father, and that is His chosen way to relate to us—as a good Father, where we can cry out for Daddy.

If we are going to talk about who God is, and if we are going to talk about His names, we must talk about Jesus. One thing we must understand about the Bible is this: everything from Genesis to Revelation points to Jesus. The purpose of telling the story of creation was for us to understand that Jesus, who is the Word in the flesh, according to John 1, is eternal. He was there with God in the beginning, and through Him, the Word, Jesus, all things were made. The purpose of telling the story of the fall of man and all the history of the Jewish people is to show the dire need for Jesus to come down and save us all. Lastly, the purpose of the New Testament and Revelation is to show us the way to be reunited with God and to show us the end of the story. In the end, Jesus gets the glory, and we get Jesus.

FOUR

WHO IS JESUS? (GLORIFIED)

The most amazing thing about the name of Jesus is that the Bible says Jesus is the name that is glorified above any other name. That is a huge statement. This is because all the names we talked about in the Old Testament describe God's nature, even the name Yahweh, which the Hebrew people held so holy and sacred that they would not say it above a whisper. Of all these names, the name of Jesus was exalted and glorified above them all. This says a lot about how God wants to be known to the world.

Throughout history, Jesus has probably been the most debated subject in history. For thousands of years, people have debated who He was and is. Some say He was just a man; some say He was a good man; some say He was a prophet; and some say He was out of his mind. But as a Christian, there are some basic things that you must understand and believe about Jesus. After all, the reason Jesus is the most debated subject in history is that everything hinges on Him.

If you could prove that Jesus was never raised from the dead, you would disprove the entirety of Christianity. Because without the resurrection, there is no Christianity. This is why Paul says in Romans that this belief is the way to be saved. "That if you confess with your mouth the Lord Jesus and believe in your heart that God has raised Him from the dead, you will be saved" (Romans 10:9 NKJV).

Jesus Is God

There is a quotation that I love that was made by one of the most influential apologetic writers in history, C. S. Lewis, in his book *Mere Christianity*. He states that Jesus did not leave the subject of His Godhood up for debate. You must either dismiss Him as a fool talking nonsense; reject Him as someone with evil intent, lying and deceiving everyone; or accept Him as exactly who He says He is. This statement is a bold attempt not to make you agree Jesus is God or prove the fact that He is. It was merely an attempt to illustrate that Jesus did not leave room for a mediocre answer to the question. He did not leave room for someone to say there is insufficient evidence to decide. The fact is, Jesus claims publicly that He is God. The religious leaders of the day wanted to kill Him for speaking it blasphemously. This tells us the same truth that C. S. Lewis explained. You cannot just take some without all. You cannot take Jesus as a teacher or a good person unless you accept Him as God.

Jesus, the Son of God

There is a moment in the New Testament that I believe reveals how Jesus wants to reveal Himself to us. This is found in Mark 16:13. Jesus took the disciples to a place called Caesarea Philippi and asked them, "Who do men say that I am?" Jesus was essentially asking them, what's the word on the street? What are people saying about me? After they rattled off a few of the most popular things people said, Jesus, probably after having a laugh with his disciples at some of the answers, asked a more personal version of the question. He asked them, who do you say I am?

Jesus was asking a question so important to Him. He wanted to know if they really understood who He was. Not because of what they heard, and not because of what they were told, but because God had revealed it to them.

At this moment, Peter, who was the most vocal about matters such as these, stood up and said with confidence, "You are the Christ, the Son of the living God" (Matthew 16:16 NKJV).

Then Jesus says something to Peter that still rings true today. "Jesus answered and said to him, 'Blessed are you, Simon Bar-Jonah, for flesh and blood has not revealed this to you, but my Father who is in heaven. And I also say to you that you are Peter, and on this rock I will build my church, and the gates of Hades shall not prevail against it'" (Matthew 16:17–18 NKJV).

Jesus was saying three really important things here. First, He made a point to say that flesh and blood did not reveal this to Peter, but the Father in heaven.

This is saying that no matter how much you read or how much you study, you cannot learn your way to a revelation of who Jesus is. As much as I love to study apologetics, this is the study of how we defend our Christian beliefs. You cannot debate or reason your way to a revelation of who Jesus is. The only way for us to know and understand who Jesus is is for us to receive a direct revelation from the Father.

Second, at the end of this verse Jesus says something interesting to me. "On this rock I will build my church, and the gates of Hades/Hell shall not prevail against it" (Matthew 16:18 NKJV). The question that comes out in this statement is, what rock is Jesus talking about? Some theologians say that when Jesus changed Simon's name to Peter, He was talking about Peter. This is the argument that justifies the papal authority over the Catholic Church. The idea is that Jesus is exalting a man as the head of the church. However, if you examine the tone in which Jesus speaks these words, the focus of the moment was not on Peter. The focus of the moment was the answer to the question that Jesus asked at the beginning of the lesson: Who do you say I am?

Peter's answer to Jesus's question is the key to everything. But it wasn't just that He had the right answer. It was how He got the right answer. My high school math teacher would be proud of this statement because it is not just that we have the answer. Many people may be able to say the words "Jesus is the Son of God," but if we are going to have power in the words Jesus is the Son of God, there must be a revelation. The rock Jesus was exalting is the ability to get a revelation about the person of Jesus from the Father. When we get that revelation, the gates of hell will not prevail against it.

This brings us to another question. Why the gates of hell? Is this saying that we are going to storm the gates of hell? Or is it even worse, that somehow the gates of hell are going to come and attack us, and we will have to battle them off like some medieval horror movie? The most interesting thing about Jesus's words here is not only in what He said but where He said it. This conversation happens at a place called Caesarea Philippi, a small city known for its temple and worship of the Greek god Pan. This was the dominant religion in the region.

When Jesus said these words, he was standing at a place where one of the largest natural springs feeding the Jordan River was located. This spring was believed to be and was commonly called the gates of hell. It was common for people to come here and make sacrifices to appease the gods, believing this well went straight down to the underworld.

Understanding this, we can look at the words of Jesus and say He wanted us to know that when we get a revelation of who Jesus is, nothing can stop the church Jesus is building—not a common thought, dominant worship, and societal movement. Nothing can tear down the church Jesus is building. As long as the church is built on the rock—the revelation from the Father that Jesus is the Son of God—it will be unstoppable. So when we have this revelation, we don't need to worry about the secular culture and political powers tearing down or stopping the spread of the gospel. Because we know that this revelation will bring us victory when we know and understand that Jesus is the Son of God, just like He said.

Jesus, Head of the Church

The third important point that Jesus makes in this passage is when He says, "On this rock, I will build my Church" (Matthew 16:18 NKJV). The idea that Jesus would make a man the head of the church was not accepted by early church believers. Jesus said it is His Church. It is all over the New Testament from the leaders of the church that Jesus is the head. And it is a fundamental belief that we need to understand.

"And he is the head of the body, the church; he is the beginning and the firstborn from among the dead, so that in everything he might have the supremacy" (Colossians 1:18 NIV).

"And God placed all things under his feet and appointed him to be head over everything for the church" (Ephesians 1:22 NIV).

"For the husband is the head of the wife as Christ is the head of the church, his body, of which he is the Savior" (Ephesians 5:23 NIV).

We need to understand the authority that Jesus gives us as we give Him Headship of the Church and our lives. If we run the show, we get whatever we can do in our own power. But if we let Jesus run the show, we get all the blessing and power that He has to offer, and His name is exalted above every name. If you want to know God, all you have to do is look at Jesus because in Him is everything we need. "For God, who said, 'Let light shine out of darkness,' made his light shine in our hearts to give us the light of the knowledge of God's glory displayed in the face of Christ" (2 Corinthians 4:6 NIV).

Jesus, Bridegroom

I will never forget the day I decided I wanted to marry my wife, Jane. I had gone to my favorite jewelry store and sat down with a designer to design the ring. I didn't want to give her just any old ring that any other woman could buy and wear. I wanted her to have something special. The truth of the matter is, I could not afford the best money could buy, but I still wanted it to be special. I still remember the moment that I gave it to her, the look on her face. I remember how proud she was to wear it, how proud I was when people saw it and said, "Wow, I have never seen a ring like that before."

When it comes to engagements, what is so special? You are really not so different from the boyfriend and girlfriend who have been dating for years. You are still not married yet. What is the big deal? The big deal is that once I gave her that ring, I gave her something along with that ring: a promise. She could look at that ring and know she had my promise that I was going to marry her, that I was going to spend my life with her, that I was going to spend my life loving only her. Also, when she put that ring on and said yes, she gave me her promise as well. Even if we had not yet said our vows or tied the knot. We had not yet said I do. But right in the middle of all of that was the promise.

This is the same promise we get when we say yes to Jesus. In Ephesians 5:22–33, Paul tells us how a woman should submit to her husband and how a husband should love his wife as Christ loved the Church. This is a beautiful picture of how Jesus feels about the Church. Jesus does not want to just be your Savior or Lord. Jesus does not want to be a distant God. He wants an intimate relationship with you—so much so that Paul tells a husband that he should love his wife, just like Christ loves the Church.

At the end of this, Paul explains more. He says I am not talking really about a husband and wife; I am talking about Christ. "This is a profound mystery—but I am talking about Christ and the church" (Ephesians 5:32 NIV).

To me, the profound mystery in this is that all through the Bible, Jesus expresses His desire to have a relationship with us. Jesus left eternity in heaven, and He came to earth to live among us for one purpose. After His death, at the end of it all, Jesus was promised one thing: the Church. The Church was His reward. He was glorified, and His name was exalted. Still, at the end of the day, He did it so that He could have a relationship again with us, just like it was in the beginning when God would walk and talk with humankind in the garden. Jesus wants to make you His bride.

So what shall we do? Repent and be baptized. Then spend the rest of your life in the promise that Jesus will come back for you and make you His bride, and He will come back for His Church that is ready and waiting for Him. He will come back for his Church that has held true to their promise that they will love Him and only Him. He will come back for His Church that did not give themselves away to any other. We spend our lives loving and preaching about Jesus and letting Him be our Lord.

Deciding to follow Jesus is the first step of many. We must first understand that the very first step was not ours, it was Jesus's. He came to us, He saved us, He made a way for us, and He made our spirit come alive. When our hearts are moved toward Jesus, and we accept Him into our lives, we can be sure that He will finish what He started. He will make us into what He wants us to be—however, we also have a role to play. We must surrender our lives to Him and let Him lead us and guide us along the way. We don't want to stay where we are but want to grow into maturity. We want to become a perfect reflection of Christ.

As you continue through this book, I encourage you to take your time to reflect on the things we discuss. Read through the scriptures and meditate on them. Pray that God will speak to you and open your eyes to see His truth. I would also encourage you to find someone who can help you, who can explain things to you, who you can feel comfortable asking any question. Find someone you can feel comfortable allowing to speak into your life. If you do this, you will move past elementary thinking and will begin to lay a foundation of faith and knowledge of God. You will have a platform to stand on that will propel you into your future with Christ. It all starts on day one, when you decide not to stay where Jesus found you, but you chose to take your first step into the family of God.

PART 2

FIVE

FOUNDATIONS

First Things First

Not too long ago I was driving down the road. I looked to the right and noticed something different. Where there used to be an open field, or a field full of construction equipment, was now a building. It seemed like this building just popped up all of a sudden, overnight even. I was amazed. How did this happen? Did I miss all the work? I could not believe how fast the growth happened when it seemed like they had set up for construction months ago, and there seemed to be people there, but there was no noticeable progress until now, and it seemed to happen all of a sudden.

When I thought about this, our walk with God is not so different. The builders were working hard the whole time; they were making progress; they were building. I just didn't notice. Before the noticeable work is done first, the builder must lay a solid foundation, which is key to constructing a nice building. It is the key to everything. If the foundation is weak, the building will crack and sag as it ages and matures. It will not keep its shape; it will not hold to the form in which it was created.

We are much like this. If we do not lay a firm and solid foundation in what we know of God, and our faith, then when people come with false teaching when life hits us with trouble, when we feel the pressures from society pressuring us to give up our convictions, we will have nothing to stand on. That is why the scriptures in the book of Hebrews tell us we need to grow in maturity not laying the foundation again (see Hebrews 6:1).

In my life, I have done a lot of remodeling and a lot of building. There are times that a house, as it ages, has some cracks and sagging. A few years ago, I went back to Indiana to visit my grandparents. They live in the house my grandfather grew up in. Over the years they expanded some of the house and added some rooms. However, they did not expand the foundation. They put it on some blocks in the front yard. They did this because the ground there is relatively dry, and they don't get much flooding in the flatland of the Midwest. Well, one year they had a record-breaking amount of rain, so much so that it started to flood. This caused the usually hard ground to become soft and muddy. I think you can see where I am going here.

To make a long story short, the blocks that were holding up the front addition of the house began to sink, and the front of the house separated from the rest. In the upstairs room, you could see the wall pull away from the house. When you walked into the room you felt the slope in the floor. There was almost a two-to-three-inch gap in some parts of the wall where the separation had begun. When I saw this, I immediately recommended to my grandfather that he call someone in to rebuild the foundation under the front of the house before his room ended up in the front yard.

But just like this house, at times it seems faster and easier to just build without regard to the foundation. However, in the case of this house, although it took many, many years to see the effect, it would have been much easier and cheaper to build the proper foundation at the beginning rather than waiting until there was a gap. To fix it, they must raise it back up, dig underneath, and undo the damage that had begun before they could begin to build again.

That is why the writer of Hebrews says, "Let us not lay the foundation again. We need to get it right the first time around so we can be grounded in our understanding so that we have something solid to build our lives on." That way, when growth happens, we will not be crushed or cracked; we will not sag or sink but will be that city that is built on top of a mountain, and all can see as we shine and display the image and glory of God.

Jesus uses the analogy of the man who built his house on the sand, and when the storm came, it was knocked down. But He talks about the man who built his house on the rock. Notice the word choice that Jesus used: rock. This is a revelation from God of who Jesus is. This man had a foundation that was solid, firm, and strong. His house stood even in the storm (see Matthew 7:24–29).

Now that we have talked about why we need a solid foundation, what does that really mean for us? There are not many places where the Bible gives us a list of things that we should know or learn. The Bible is filled with stories, history, and letters. But in those letters, it is uncommon for the writers to give us a list of doctrines or lessons. In Hebrews, however, the writer gives us just that: "Therefore let us move beyond the elementary teachings about Christ and be taken forward to maturity, not laying again the foundation of repentance from acts that lead to death, and of faith in God, instruction about cleansing rites, the laying on of hands, the resurrection of the dead, and eternal judgment" (Hebrews 6:1–2 NIV).

Here in scripture we have a unique list that the author gives us and says if you want to lay a foundation, lay it once. We don't want to have to come back to this over and over again. Why? Because you have a house to build. And your house will take you all your life to complete, and you don't have time to go back and fix the foundation because every moment that you lay the foundation again, you miss out on something new. So what is on the list?

Once we have moved past the elementary teachings about Jesus, we can lay the foundation of

- Repentance from acts that lead to death;
- Faith in God;
- Water baptism;
- Laying on of hands;
- The resurrection of the dead; and
- Eternal judgment.

If these things seem new to you, that's great! I want to help you lay down a foundational understanding of these things in your life. If this list looks scary to you, don't worry. As the Holy Spirit is working in you even now, He will be the one who ultimately teaches you about these truths, not through knowledge, not through human learning, but through your heart and spirit. All I am doing is opening the door so that you can see into the other side, and you can then begin that journey with the Spirit into growth and a new future in Christ. As we go through this list, I am going to go in the order the author wrote it. I believe sometimes that God cares about the how as much as the what, and the author by the inspiration of the Holy Spirit set this order so we will follow it here.

SIX

REPENTANCE

There are two different Greek words used in the New Testament that are usually translated as *repent*. Fist is *"metamelomai."* A word that denotes a feeling of regret or remorse. The second is *"metanoeo or metanoia"* This words denotes not only a change of mind but also a change of purpose. It is not just regretting what was done, but it is a change that affects all decisions and thoughts that will be made in the future. This is the word that is most often use when the forgiveness of sins is promised. The reason I bring this up is that one is what is required of us in the sanctification process in our walk with Christ. The other is more like human emotion. However, before I go much further, I want to be clear with one fundamental principle that we must understand. This statement I am about to make might shake some theology that you may have acquired over the years of hearing about the Christian faith. Some of that is because of the way I will say it, but a lot of it comes from a false perception of true salvation.

Repentance is *not* a requirement for salvation.

Before you throw this book away because now you believe me to be a heretic, let me explain. It is taught all through the Bible that salvation is not about what we do. Salvation is not by works. Salvation is not something that we can earn. We love these statements because they ring true to the essence of grace. So if salvation is purely a work of Christ and cannot be earned by anything that we do, and there is no act that can make us worthy of grace, then we must include the act of repentance to that list. Don't get me wrong; repentance is enormously important on our walk with Christ. But it is just not a requirement for us to receive the gift of salvation.

According to many of the writers of scripture, we see that no act can make us more deserving of grace. In John 6:44 John writes that no one can come to

Jesus unless he or she is first drawn by the Father. In Ephesians 2:1–10 Paul describes a picture of us in our sin and transgressions. He says that we are dead in our transgressions. That is a perfect picture of us before salvation.

Sin does not make you bad. Sin makes you dead. The reason Paul uses the word *dead* is that dead people cannot do anything. Salvation is the act of Jesus that makes us come alive. It is impossible for a dead person to repent. It is impossible for dead people to do anything because they are dead. Paul continues and says that while you were dead and could do nothing, Jesus did everything and made you alive. "But because of his great love for us, God, who is rich in mercy, made us alive with Christ even when we were dead in transgressions—it is by grace you have been saved" (Ephesians 2:4–5 NIV).

How was this done? By grace, because of His great love for us. God made you alive with Christ. Understanding this is vitally important. It was so important that the writer of Hebrews puts it on the list of six fundamental truths that must be understood. And it is all wrapped up in this last statement: "For it is by grace you have been saved, through faith—and this is not from yourselves, it is the gift of God—not by works, so that no one can boast" (Ephesians 2:8–9).

Now that we have discussed what repentance is not, what is it? The word *repentance* in most people's minds is the act of being sorry and turning away from sin. Growing up in church I have often heard people attempt to describe repentance as turning away from sin, doing a 180-degree turn and walking away from it. Although this is not all wrong—repentance is closely associated with godly sorrow and does evoke change. This is not the precise definition of repentance according to the Bible.

According to Paul as he writes to the Corinthians, there is a difference between godly sorrow and worldly sorrow. "Godly sorrow brings repentance that leads to salvation and leaves no regret, but worldly sorrow brings death" (2 Corinthians 7:10 NIV).

Now we know repentance is not being sorry. Being sorry leads us to repentance, but it is not repentance itself. The word repentance in the Bible, most clearly defined by scripture, means to have a change of mind. So as much as repentance is not just being sorry, it is also not just not sinning. It is more than knowing something is wrong and choosing not to do that anymore. It is a complete change of mind. This verse wonderfully explains the revolutionary power of repentance. "Do not conform to the pattern of this world, but be transformed by the renewing of your mind. Then you will be able to test and approve what God's will is—his good, pleasing and perfect will" (Romans 12:2 NIV).

Paul writes a contrasting view against conformity to the world. When we are part of the world, we see things the world's way. Before we were saved by grace, we did not have the mind of Christ. But after Jesus saves us, He tells us that we are born by the Spirit. After Jesus brings us to new life through salvation, we then must have a change of mind. We must allow our minds to be transformed. Into what? Into a person who thinks like Jesus. And we do this how? By the renewing of our mind. This is repentance. We change our view, we change our mind, and we no longer follow the pattern the world gave us. We now follow the pattern that Jesus gave us. This is the beginning process of sanctification. This is why, when the people asked Peter, "What shall we do?", he answered them: first repent and then be baptized.

To finish off our illustration of repentance, I want to tell you a story of a pivotal moment in the lives of two men. Both were followers of Christ. Both were His disciples. Both walked with Him for His entire ministry on Earth. Both men sinned and failed and felt sorry for their sins.

But only one man found repentance.

The first man is Peter, earlier known as Simon before Jesus changed his name. Peter was proud and boasted of his love for Jesus. He made all sorts of promises, but Jesus predicted his failure. After Jesus was arrested in the garden, Peter ran and hid. In the courtyard he was asked if he was a follower of Christ. At this moment Peter denied him. He was asked three times, the last by a young child. To bring weight to his denial he cursed as he yelled that he did not know Jesus. Just then, Peter heard the rooster crow, and he remembered the words of Jesus when He said that he would deny Jesus three times before the rooster crowed. After this he went outside, and the Bible says he wept bitterly (see Matthew 26:69–75).

The second man is Judas, the keeper of the money who struggled with greed. He often made poor decisions when money was involved. The night before Jesus died at the last supper, Jesus dipped the bread together with Judas and predicted his betrayal. He told Judas to go and do what he was going to do and do it quickly. Most who heard did not understand what Jesus meant, but Judas left that place and went to the priests and made a deal with them that he would betray Jesus for thirty pieces of silver. It is likely that Judas did not really know what they were going to do to Jesus when they found Him as when Judas found out that Jesus was condemned to die, he felt great sorrow for what he had done. He went back to the priests and told them that he had sinned and caused an innocent man to be condemned. It was then that he threw the silver pieces he had received on the ground and left (see Matthew 27:3–10).

What was the difference between these two men? One left his place of sorrow and found himself in repentance. Jesus came to Peter and told him to "feed my sheep" (John 21:17). Peter then went on to be the first person to preach the gospel after the day of Pentecost and thousands were added to the kingdom.

The other left his place of sorrow and fell into a depression. He went from that place to a field and hung himself because he could not bear to feel the condemnation and guilt from his sin.

Do you think the death of Christ was not big enough or strong enough for Judas? No! On the contrary. Jesus showed many times his love for Judas, even when Jesus knew he would betray Him. Do you think that if Judas would have come to the feet of Jesus after his betrayal that He would have treated Judas any differently than the thief on the cross? Of course not!

If both men were offered salvation, and both men felt sorrow, why then did they get different results? It was because Peter, unlike Judas, was able to find repentance in the renewal of his mind. He changed his thinking. He did not look at his sin with guilt and condemnation, he saw his sin as an opportunity for grace. This is what was meant when Paul penned the words, "Godly sorrow brings repentance that leads to salvation and leaves no regret, but worldly sorrow brings death" (2 Corinthians 7:10 NIV).

At the end of the day, when we sin, we do not need to feel guilt, condemnation, or regret. Rather, when we sin, all we need to do is look to Jesus. The world says when you sin, you need to change. When you sin, you need to fix yourself and clean yourself up.

Jesus says when you sin, look to Him, and He will clean you up. This is true repentance. This is what God requires from us. This is what brings a true change in our lives. When we change our thinking from *I need to be good enough, I need to change, I need to stop sinning, and I need to be better* to *All I need is Jesus, and once I have Him, He will begin a work in me that will change me to be more like him, in His time. He will turn my ashes into beauty, He will make my past a testimony, and He will take my filthy rags and turn them into righteousness,* this is true repentance.

SEVEN

FAITH IN GOD

Once we understand repentance, we can begin to look at the idea of faith. Until our minds are focused on Christ, it is impossible to have faith, and without faith, it is impossible to please God. To get started in talking about faith in God, I want to tell you what it is. Then I can tell you a little more about what it isn't.

Faith, in biblical terms, basically means trust. There are many verses that come to mind that pull this all together. You may have heard this one: we live by faith, not by sight (2 Corinthians 5:7). There are faith statements all over the Bible. We certainly cannot talk about faith without bringing up this one: "Now faith is confidence in what we hope for and assurance about what we do not see" (Hebrews 11:1 NIV).

Listen to the tone and the words the writer of Hebrews chose to use—words such as confidence and assurance. Here is another place we see faith: "Now to the one who works, wages are not credited as a gift but as an obligation. However, to the one who does not work but trusts God who justifies the ungodly, their faith is credited as righteousness" (Romans 4:4–5 NIV).

What a wonderful picture. If we work for our salvation, we get what we deserve. According to Romans 3:23, the wages of sin is death. So at our best, on our best day, the best we can get is death. However, to the one who does not work but trusts, that sentence is one of the most theologically profound statements in the Bible. Human religion says we must work to get to God. Jesus says the one who does not work but trusts. Not just trust in anything but in God, the one who justifies the ungodly. Their faith is credited as righteousness. Now to unpack that and put it in simple vernacular, this is saying that we are not saved by what we can do, we are saved because we trust in what God has done. And the trust that we have in God is just like if we were perfect and without sin.

To wrap this up, many times we look at faith as hope. We say the words, "I have faith," but often that translates in our hearts as, "I hope this works." Faith is not simply believing. Faith goes beyond belief. Faith is like looking at a clock and being able to say that when the short hand goes past one number, one hour has passed. You may hear that and say, "Yeah, everyone knows that." But if you had never seen a clock work before, you may not have so much faith. Faith is not hope, it is the substance or the confidence in what is hoped for. It is not belief in something we cannot see. It is the evidence or assurance of what we cannot see.

Now that we know what faith is, let's apply it to our Christian walk. When we say we have faith in God, what are we really talking about? We are saying we trust Him, but trust Him to do what? There are many promises in the Bible, and many have already come true. But at the end of the day, there is one promise that we are all looking for, or at least we should be: when Jesus comes back to take us to heaven to live with Him.

Faith is what gets us through the tough days. Faith is what gets us through when the miracle doesn't come. Faith is what keeps us going when every evil power of this world is coming after you. Faith is what keeps our chin up when everything seems to keep beating it down. This is so because we know that this life is temporary. We know that this is not our home. We know Jesus said those who endure persecution will have a great reward in heaven. We know that no matter what happens here on earth, my future is Jesus.

When we have that kind of faith, we have assurance that God has a plan for the long arc of our life. Though in the short term we may feel trouble, we know that in the long term, God will overcome. When we have faith enough to know that God is sovereign, and nothing can stop his plans to the point that we understand that even our enemies work for God and will always accomplish His will. When we have that kind of faith, we please God. "And without faith it is impossible to please God, because anyone who comes to him must believe that he exists and that he rewards those who earnestly seek him" (Hebrews 11:6 NIV).

If my faith pleases God, what happens when I lose it? So many times we are faced with circumstances that are too hard to bear. There are times we just lose faith. There are times we can't see God through the cloud of our pain. At this moment, is God displeased with us? Will He leave us? Will we suddenly no longer have the promise? Not at all. The only reason we can have faith is that He is always faithful to His word. God said, "I will never leave you or forsake you" (Deuteronomy 31:6). This is echoed in the New Testament in Hebrews 13, where the writer says God will never leave us or forsake us, so why should we be afraid of what mere mortals can do to us? Lastly, Paul writes these wonderful words to Timothy to encourage him: "If we are faithless, he remains faithful, for he cannot disown himself" (2 Timothy 2:13 NIV).

I thank God for this verse, as we all lose faith at times. We find ourselves in a place where we trust our own way over God's way. With all this we can know that no matter where you go, no matter what you do, God is always with you, and God will never leave you. Even if we have no faith, He is still faithful. Believing this is the greatest faith.

EIGHT

BAPTISM IN WATER

This brings us to the next foundation on our list, baptism. When I married my wife, Jane, we did what all couples do at the end of the ceremony. After we exchanged our vows, we gave each other a ring. The wonderful thing about the rings that are exchanged is that they are a symbol of our love for each other. To even go further, it is a declaration to everyone who sees my finger that I am hers and she is mine.

Baptism in water is much like this. To fully understand baptism, we need to look at the Bible and how it was written. The Bible is broken down into two sections: the Old Testament and the New Testament. Have you ever wondered what this means? The word *testament* literally means *covenant*. That is a word that has much more meaning, even if you don't study the Bible. So we have the old covenant, and we have the new covenant. A covenant is like a bond or agreement, a contract in a sense. But it goes much deeper than a contract like the ones we use today, where if you pay enough money you can get out of it, or if you can find a loophole you can break it. This is a deep-seated contract backed by eternal promise with the Almighty God.

Whenever there is a contract, there is always a binding factor. You may add a signature or seal, something that says I will honor this and here is the proof. In the old covenant that God made with Abraham, the contract was sealed with circumcision (see Genesis 17:10). This was so important to God.

In Exodus 4:24 Moses recounts a story after God called him to go back to Egypt. He, his wife, and his son began to travel. Moses knew God's covenant command and so did his wife, but they chose not to follow. With this decision, they were out of the covenant promise with God. So God came in the night to kill Moses. When his wife saw this, she quickly grabbed a flint knife and circumcised her son and touched Moses's feet with the foreskin, and said, "Surely you are the bridegroom of blood to me." In this, she was speaking of circumcision.

When we look at this from the perspective of a covenant relationship, this is exactly what baptism is. Jesus began a new covenant with us through His death, burial, and resurrection. When God draws us through godly sorrow through repentance, we put our faith in Jesus. We enter a covenant relationship with Him, and the seal or sign of this covenant is baptism. We see this clearly in Colossians 2:11–15. The truth is that there is nowhere in scripture that allows or even considers an unbaptized Christian. It was just something that the early believers would never think of.

What Is Baptism, and Why Should We Do It?

As a parent, I get asked a fundamental question every day. I will have to admit, it is an annoying question as a parent, but I understand the need for it. The question is why? With every command or request I give my kids, I always get this question. As much as we may hate it, it is necessary. If you don't understand this, even your next question will be the same: why? Here is why we need the why. The why gives meaning, purpose, and power. Without the why, the what is insignificant. Without the why we perform meaningless acts of servitude. And as we talked about at the beginning of this book, God did not create us for mindless servitude. He created us for a relationship with Him, for Him, and to Him, and to spread His image. He wants us to understand and choose.

So now to our question. Why should I be baptized? First, we should be baptized because we are following Christ's example. In Matthew 3:13–17 we see a beautiful picture of baptism. Jesus comes down to John the Baptist and says, "I need you to baptize me." John reluctantly agrees, and then Jesus goes into the water. As He comes out of the water, the Spirit of God comes down and rests on Him. The voice of the Father comes from heaven affirming Him and His calling.

The first question that comes to my mind is: if baptism is only for repentance of sin, why did Jesus get baptized? Jesus never sinned, He was perfect, right? Jesus did this because baptism is designed for us to identify with Christ. When Jesus came to be baptized, what He was saying was, "I want to identify with you."

The next reason we should be baptized is to be obedient to God. Jesus said in Matthew 3:15, "I need you to do this so that I can fulfill all righteousness." Jesus wanted us to understand that baptism was a command from God. This was the seal of the covenant. But also, how can we say we love God and want to give Him our lives but don't want to identify with Him? No, this was so important to Jesus that He included it in the great commission. "Therefore go and make disciples of all nations, baptizing them in the name of the Father and of the Son and of the Holy Spirit" (Matthew 28:19 NIV).

In baptism, we are also united with the body of Christ. This is what unifies us in the faith. "Make every effort to keep the unity of the Spirit through the bond of peace. There is one body and one Spirit, just as you were called to one hope when you were called; one Lord, one faith, one baptism; one God and Father of all, who is over all and through all and in all" (Ephesians 4:3–6 NIV).

Baptism here is put on such a high level. It is so clear that it is important to God that we are baptized. This means God already did the work in your heart, and baptism is the celebration of what God has done through Jesus.

Baptism is not required for salvation. Again, I want to emphasize that we are saved by faith alone, not by any works of man so that we can boast. Your salvation does not come from baptism; however, it is a huge part of our Christian walk. This is the first thing that sets us apart, the initial way that we identify publicly with Christ and His church. Without this, we are just someone who believes in God and the Bible says in the book of James. "You believe that there is one God. Good! Even the demons believe that—and shudder" (James 2:19 NIV).

Though baptism is not required for salvation, it is immensely important for us to walk this Christian life in victory.

How Should We Be Baptized?

This is an age-old question and debated in the church: How should we be baptized? In order to fully answer that, we have to look at what baptism represents. Baptism is an illustration of the gospel.

It is a representation of Jesus's death, His burial, and resurrection by His own power. This is the image that baptism celebrates. We Identify with His death, our old nature is gone, and we bury the old nature of sin that we were born with as Christ gives us new life and new birth. However, we do not stay dead but are resurrected with new life. This is the picture that we portray when we are baptized.

To properly explain how we should be baptized, I would have to sum up hundreds of years of Church history. There has been much debate on this subject. I am going to show you what I believe to be the most biblical form of baptism. But I would encourage you, if you are looking for more information on this, please study, go see one of your church leaders, find someone grounded in faith to walk you through this process.

The most biblical form of baptism that I can find in scripture is full immersion. We see this when Jesus was baptized in Matthew 3. Jesus went into and came out of the water. We also see this in Acts 8:36–38, where Philip baptized the Ethiopian eunuch and they stopped by the road. They went into and came out of the water. Full immersion also gives the closest representation of the picture of the gospel—being buried and identifying with the burial and then being resurrected.

I also believe the Bible teaches that we must be born again to be baptized. Not just born. Many churches and organizations practice infant baptism, but I believe it to be clear in Colossians 2:11–12 that baptism is circumcision of the heart, and it is circumcision that is not done by human hands. The old covenant was a physical birth into a physical community with a physical sign which was circumcision of the body. The new covenant is a spiritual birth into a spiritual community with a spiritual sign which is baptism in water. Thus, just as circumcision was done eight days after an infant was born, so too baptism should happen as soon as you have been born again. This was what John was talking about when he wrote the following: "Yet to all who did receive him, to those who believed in his name, he gave the right to become children of God— children born not of natural descent, nor of human decision or a husband's will, but born of God" (John 1:12–13 NIV).

If you are asking, "What shall I do?" You need to repent, change your thinking, and be baptized, and identify with Christ in His death and resurrection. Be united with the body of Christ and the Church. When you do this, you will allow the power of the Holy Spirit to begin a work in you that will tear away the old person you used to be. You will no longer identify with sin, but you will identify with the resurrection power of Christ. Then, you can trust and have faith in Jesus's name because you have seen Him work and have the promise under the new covenant as we walk in a covenant relationship with Him.

NINE

THE LAYING ON OF HANDS

❖❖❖❖❖❖

The Baptism in the Holy Spirit

Growing up as a Pentecostal kid in church I saw a lot of things, some good, some not so good. As a kid, you learn quickly that there is humor in all sorts of things. Especially in a Pentecostal church. One of the things I remember clearly is how Pentecostal pastors would do altar calls. They brought everyone down to the front of the church and lay hands on them. I learned from a young age that you might want to think twice before going down to the altar and letting them lay hands on you, because in most cases you were going to end up on the floor. As a young child, I didn't really understand what was going on. People fell, shook on the floor, laughed uncontrollably, cried, or sang. It seemed like if you went down there you never knew what could happen next.

I remember the first time I got the courage to go down to the altar. I was ready, I thought. I was finally at the place where I had decided I wanted God to touch me too. I wanted God to work in me, and I didn't care how foolish I looked. I boldly got up out of my seat and walked down that aisle. When I made it to the front, I stood there with my arms in the air just waiting for God to blast me. I'll never forget this day. As I stood there, the evangelist walked by me almost as if in passing, put his hand on my head, said a short prayer, and moved on.

I was just left there wondering what happened. Or more rightly stated, what didn't happen? I was left with all sorts of questions. Did I do it wrong? Was I thinking about the wrong thing? *Maybe God doesn't want to touch me. Maybe my hands were not high enough.* I had heard so many talks and sermons about how all we have to do is ask. We have not because we ask not, right? So here I was, left questioning.

Months went by, a year went by, and I started to think there was something wrong with me. I was seeing others being filled with the Holy Spirit, and oh, I wanted it too. I saw others do things that I thought were so wonderful: speaking in tongues, healing, singing, crying, worshiping, delivering, and prophesying.

After a while, I just listened to what other people were saying, and I repeated their words. I sat close to a man or woman in our prayer services so I could hear him or her speak in tongues, and I repeated what he or she said until eventually I believed I was actually speaking in tongues.

I remember the first time my dad heard me speaking someone else's words. He was so excited that his son was speaking in tongues. At least from my perspective that was what he was excited about. I continued this way through high school and into college, all the while knowing deep in my heart that I had accepted a fake, an imitation as the real infilling of the Spirit.

It wasn't long after starting college that I became disillusioned with the idea of speaking in tongues. I knew in my heart that what I had was not real. I believed it existed, but maybe it wasn't for me. I believed in the Bible, but I just didn't know how to get there. So one day, alone in my room, I prayed to God. I said, "God, I am done faking it, and I will never speak in tongues again until you move my lips, until I am trying to speak in English and something else comes out." I would like to say at that moment God filled me with the Holy Spirit and reaffirmed in me that He is real and that He wants to give us His Holy Spirit. But that was not how it happened. I just always prayed in English.

What was the problem? Why didn't God want to give me what I saw Him give so many others? Why didn't God want to give me what I read about in the Bible so many times? It all came down to one moment. There was a second moment in my life that like the first I will never forget. It was when I felt the power of the Holy Spirit for the first time for real. I was in a worship service at Hillsong Church in Sydney, Australia. It was life as usual for me. We were at what they called at the time Touching Heaven Night. This was basically a night where they came together and worshiped and invited people to come to the altar to be prayed for.

They would pray for healing, deliverance, and all sorts of things. Essentially it was just like how it sounded. They wanted to touch heaven.

As a college student I went to every service available, so I was there, in my seat worshiping. I didn't go down for prayer; I didn't ask for anything, but for some reason that day I was engrossed in worship. All I wanted was to worship Jesus and feel His presence. As I stood there worshiping, I looked down and I saw a man in a wheelchair making his way to the front for prayer. This was a usual sight. He came to every single one of these, and every month he came down for prayer. This man was in a powered wheelchair, and he could not move any part of his body except his head. He had a headband wrapped around his chin with a rod on it that he could use to push the button to make his chair move.

All of a sudden I felt a rush of power that I had never felt before. I felt like my body was on fire. It was like I was frozen in a moment; the world stood still, and I was there with fire in my bones. I honestly don't know if I said anything at all, and to be frank I didn't care. At that moment it was not about the tongue or the manifestation of the Spirit. It was about the Spirit

Himself. For the first time in my life, I felt the Spirit of God flowing through me.

Then the Spirit spoke to me. God told me in what seemed like an audible voice because it was so clear what He wanted me to do. He said as I looked at that man in the wheelchair, "If you pray for him, I will heal him." I wish I could tell you that I instantly ran out of my seat and lay my hands on this man, and he began walking and leaping and praising God. But unfortunately, this is not that kind of story. This is a story of my continuous lack of understanding and disobedience.

I still remember this moment like it was yesterday because this moment changed my life forever. I remember the fire, I remember the voice, I remember the feeling of power in my bones, and I remember the moment that I spoke. I said to God in my heart, "But God, I am just a first-year Bible college student, and these men are seasoned pastors. What will they think if I just walk down there and pray for this man?"

Then, as fast as it came, the Spirit left. I still come to tears when I think of it. I felt so cold and alone, so empty and ashamed. I begged God, "Please, come back, I will do it, I will go pray for him." But I just had this feeling in my heart that said it was too late.

That day I made a new promise to God. It had nothing to do with speaking in tongues or how I would feel. It had nothing to do with what I would receive. I said to Him, "I will never question You again. No matter what You ask, I will do it. No matter how strange it sounds or how foolish I will look, I will do it." Because I never wanted to feel that empty ever again.

As I have grown older and God has given me a greater understanding, I have learned more about His Spirit. The problem I had was that I could not see past the manifestation of the Spirit. I was not seeking the Spirit; I was seeking the manifestations. I wanted the visible signs, the gift, with no regard for the giver. I want to take you through a few simple truths in the scriptures about the baptism of the Holy Spirit and why we have it and what it is all about. This is what I learned from my lack of understanding and disobedience.

The Holy Spirit is not something we possess. It possesses us.

> But the manifestation of the Spirit is given to each one for the profit of all: for to one is given the word of wisdom through the Spirit, to another the word of knowledge through the same Spirit, to another faith by the same Spirit, to another gifts of healings by the same Spirit, to another the working of miracles, to another prophecy, to another discerning of spirits, to another different kinds of tongues, to another the interpretation of tongues. But one and the same Spirit works all these things, distributing to each one individually as He wills. (1 Corinthians 12:7–11 NKJV)

If we are going to seek the Spirit, we should not seek the manifestation of the Spirit. In this verse, Paul says that the Spirit works all these things, distributing to each one as He wills. This means that we do not get the ability or right to decide what gift we would like to operate in. We get the privilege of the Holy Spirit living inside of us and using us as He sees fit.

"For prophecy never came by the will of man, but holy men of God spoke as they were moved by the Holy Spirit" (2 Peter 1:21 NKJV).

"And they were all filled with the Holy Spirit and began to speak with other tongues, as the Spirit gave them utterance" (Acts 2:4 NKJV).

The main purpose of the filling of the Holy Spirit is for the Gospel to be preached with boldness: "And when they had prayed, the place where they were assembled together was shaken; and they were all filled with the Holy Spirit, and they spoke the word of God with boldness" (Act 4:31 NKJV).

This scripture is just after Peter and John had gone to the temple courts and healed the lame man sitting outside the gate called Beautiful. The Bible says that this man came with them into the temple courts walking and leaping and praising God. This was an amazing day. Many people came to them and heard the gospel and believed and were baptized. After all this, the religious leaders came and threatened them, saying, "Do not speak the name of Jesus anymore." Peter and John left that place and met up with the rest of the believers. They told them what had happened and the threats they received. Then they prayed and the Spirit came down and filled the room and shook it. What did they do? They spoke the word of God with boldness.

On the day of Pentecost (see Acts 2), the followers of Christ were in the upper room, and the Spirit of God fell on them and they were filled with the Holy Spirit. There were manifestations of tongues, walking around like drunk men, and everyone around could see it. Then Peter did something extraordinary, something that he was not able to do in his own strength. The same man who denied Christ before a child stood up and proclaimed the gospel of Jesus to the very people who had him crucified. The most amazing and miraculous thing that happened was that the Bible says each person there, from every nation, heard the disciples speaking in their native tongue.

The tongue here was not to edify themselves or about what they could receive, it was about the ability for every single person who could hear them speak to be able to clearly hear the message of the gospel. And what happened next? Thousands of people came to Jesus and were baptized.

The baptism of the Holy Spirit is a "nonnegotiable." Imagine for a moment that you were one of the twelve disciples. You walked with Jesus. You sat under His teaching every day. You saw Him do miracles and were there when He changed water to wine. You were there when Lazarus was raised from the dead. You saw every moment of it. You were in the group that Jesus sent out and came back with the report that even the demons had to obey you. You were at the last supper, you saw Him die, and you were there when He rose again. You were next to Thomas when he put his finger in the holes in his hands and touched His side. You were there when He was transfigured on the mountain, and you were there when He ascended back into heaven. You heard the words of the great commission to go into all the world and preach the gospel. You were an eyewitness to it all.

Now let me ask you this question. Do you think that everything I just said there would qualify you to go and complete the great commission? Do you think all of that would qualify you to go and spread the good news of the gospel to the world? *No!* It doesn't!

When Jesus was about to leave the planet, He said these profound words to His disciples: "On one occasion, while he was eating with them, he gave them this command: 'Do not leave Jerusalem, but wait for the gift my Father promised, which you have heard me speak about'" (Acts1:4 NIV).

This was a command! Don't leave, stay here, and wait until you have received the gift from the Father. So what was this gift? Why would Jesus say this? He makes it clear a few verses down: "But you will receive power when the Holy Spirit comes on you; and you will be my witnesses in Jerusalem, and in all Judea and Samaria, and to the ends of the earth" (Acts 1:8 NIV).

Jesus says wait! Don't go anywhere until you receive the power of the Holy Spirit, and then you will be my witnesses. That statement is profound. They could not do it without the Holy Spirit. And Jesus never intended them to. According to Jesus, the Holy Spirit is a nonnegotiable; you cannot do anything without Him.

We cannot talk about the Holy Spirit without talking about the laying on of hands. If power is the what, the Holy Spirit is the who, laying on of hands is the how. There are three different ways that I have found where the act of laying on of hands is used in the New Testament. One is healing. Jesus says in Mark 16:18 that one of the signs that will follow those who believe is that they will lay hands on the sick and they will recover. This is shown also a few times in Jesus's ministry. We see the laying on of hands for healing in Acts 28:8 and Mark 5:23. Although this is something that was talked about and was practiced, it was not always the case that the laying on of hands was needed for healing.

There are many cases in the Bible where people were healed by different processes. I think Jesus loves up-close ministry; it was His preferred method. He would often go to where the sick people were to heal them. We see this in the way Jesus chose to redeem us. He could have redeemed us without coming to Earth. He is God, after all. Still, He chose to come down from heaven to Earth right where we are to die for us. Jesus likes up-close ministry.

Though healing is a big part of the Christian life, when we talk about the foundation of the doctrine of laying on of hands, I believe this to be focused on the other two methods. The other two ways that I see the laying on of hands used in the New Testament are the appointment to a position of ministry and the infilling or baptism of the Holy Spirit.

In Acts 8:14–18, Peter and John were sent to Samaria because they heard the Samaritan people had accepted Jesus. When they got there, they asked the Samarians if they had been filled with the Holy Spirit. The Samarians replied they didn't even know there was a Holy Spirit. After hearing this, Peter and John went around laying hands on people, baptizing them into the Holy Spirit. It was so evident to onlookers that the avenue in which the Holy Spirit was given was the laying on of the apostles' hands. Simon, a magician, came to them and offered them money to have this ability.

They rebuked him for the question. My point is that in the early church this is how they received the gift of the Holy Spirit. It was by the laying on of hands. Another time we see this is when Paul writes to Timothy: "For this reason, I remind you to fan into flame the gift of God, which is in you through the laying on of my hands" (2 Timothy 1:6 NIV).

This is showing us that Timothy received the gift of the Holy Spirit from the laying on of Paul's hands. We know this is talking about the Holy Spirit because of the next verse. It says, "For the Spirit God gave us does not make us timid" (2 Timothy 1:7 NIV). This reaffirms the purpose of the Holy Spirit that we discussed earlier. Paul was writing to Timothy, saying, "Don't be timid, don't be quiet, I know the Spirit of God is in you because I was there and laid my hands on you." Paul was telling Timothy, "Don't let your gift grow cold, but rather speak boldly the gospel of Christ." There are many other scriptures in the book of Acts that talk about how the baptism of the Holy Spirit is given by the laying on of hands, and I would encourage you to read the book of Acts in your own time. There are so many things we can learn from the example of the early Church and the apostles.

The third way we see the laying on of hands used in scripture is for the appointing of people to positions of ministry. There are many types of ministries. However, some are appointed. These are what many will call the five-fold ministry. They get this name from when Paul gives us a list of five ministries or gifts that are given to edify the church. "So Christ himself gave the apostles, the prophets, the evangelists, the pastors, and teachers" (Ephesians 4:11 NIV).

We have a list of five positions of ministry that Christ Himself gave to the Church: apostles, prophets, evangelists, pastors, and teachers. The keywords here are *Christ Himself gave*. This means that if you are to move into one of these positions in the church, you must be first called, then chosen, and then appointed. I know this is not popular teaching in the church today. Many people who claim many of these positions are self-appointed. I am not saying they are bad people; I am just saying that the way they took the position of ministry is unbiblical. Meaning it does not line up with the practices we see from the leaders modeled for us in the Bible. Let me give you a few examples.

Stephen

"This proposal pleased the whole group. They chose Stephen, a man full of faith and of the Holy Spirit; also Philip, Procorus, Nicanor, Timon, Parmenas, and Nicolas from Antioch, a convert to Judaism. They presented these men to the apostles, who prayed and laid their hands on them" (Acts 6:5–6 NIV).

These men were called by God and chosen and appointed by the elders. And what did they do? They brought them in and lay hands on them. The laying on of hands here was the impartation of the spiritual gift that they had been called to. They were anointed for the work. So many times, pastors and churches fail because they are working outside of their anointing.

Paul and Barnabas

"While they were worshiping the Lord and fasting, the Holy Spirit said, 'Set apart for me Barnabas and Saul for the work to which I have called them.' So after they had fasted and prayed, they placed their hands on them and sent them off" (Acts 13:2–3 NIV).

This has the same pattern. The Holy Spirit called them, and He set them apart. Then the other apostles and leaders lay their hands on them and sent them out for the work God had called them to fulfill. Again, this was not the calling they wanted to fulfill. This was the calling God chose for them through the Holy Spirit.

Timothy

"Until I come, devote yourself to the public reading of Scripture, to preaching and to teaching. Do not neglect your gift, which was given you through prophecy when the body of elders laid their hands on you" (1 Timothy 4:13–14 NIV).

Again, we have the same pattern. Paul is telling Timothy to read the scriptures publicly, preach, and teach. He was not given this authority by Paul. He was given this authority by prophecy when the elders came together and did what? Lay their hands on him. Again, I know it is a popular thing to have people come in and say, "I am a prophet." I am always wary of these people. Not because they are bad people, but because they are not following biblical instructions. And it may be that they have been appointed as a prophet by the elders and maybe they did lay hands on them. But I want to know that this has happened before I let them speak. Why? Because the Bible says that we should judge those who are working in the ministry. Yes, I said the repulsive J-word. But it's true. It says we will know them by their fruit (Matthew 7:17–20). Paul also tells the Corinthians to judge the word of the prophets (1 Corinthians 14:29).

Positions of ministry should be appointed by leaders in the church and called by God, and this calling should be confirmed by the elders of the church by the power of the Holy Spirit. This is the way it is modeled for us in the Bible. And all this is done by the laying on of hands.

Paul also tells Timothy to be careful not to be too quick in the laying on of hands (see 1 Timothy 5:22). Why does Paul say this? Because of the weight that they put on the appointment of people to ministry positions. He basically told Timothy, "Don't just appoint people flippantly. Be sure they are called, be sure God is in it. Pray and ask the Holy Spirit to guide you in who to appoint and who to say no to." Paul understood the importance of appointment and the laying on of hands. And he said don't take it lightly because if they are not of God, if they are not really called, if they are false prophets, if they are false teachers, you will take part in their sins, and it will defile your reputation and calling.

God appoints people not based on need but on His will. He will not appoint someone just because a position is open. He will only appoint and call

Rick Cummins

someone if their heart is right with Him and they have
been filled with the Spirit and called to that calling.
So do not be quick to accept a position, but be sure
you have been called and anointed to that position. If
you are not, you cannot be successful because you are
living contrary to the Bible and working outside your
anointing.

I want to make a distinction. My statement that says
you cannot be successful must be measured regarding
what God would consider successful. It would be
totally possible for someone operating outside of
biblical truth to have a large church. It would be totally
possible for someone operating outside of biblical truth
to have a lot of money and influence. These are things
that the world would consider successful, however,
God does not judge us by these things. God judges
the heart; He judges what cannot be seen. He judges
eternal influence and eternal change. So when we look
at success, be sure to look to the Spirit, and He will
guide you to success.

TEN

THE RESURRECTION OF THE DEAD

--------◆◆◆◆◆◆--------

How Does the Story End?

Have you ever watched a suspenseful movie, one that keeps you guessing, that you just can't seem to get ahead of or keeps you on the edge of your seat? The only reason you are on the edge of your seat is that you don't know how it ends. If we know the ending, it takes all the suspense out of it. If we know that in the end the hero saves the day, marries the girl, and they ride off into the sunset, it ruins the suspense. That makes the scene where the hero has his back up against the wall and is facing imminent doom with no way out just a really cool action sequence.

This is the same experience that we can have in life. Have you ever wondered why some mature Christians seem to always be calm and full of joy, even when it seems like everything is falling apart? Have you ever wondered why some people can face the most trying circumstances and through it all raise their hands and thank God for all His blessings? Humanly speaking this seems impossible. We would look at these people from a human perspective and say they are just internalizing their pain. They are faking it. We would tell them things like, "It's not good to hold things in; you have to let it out or it will kill you." And don't get me wrong. All of that is true sometimes.

I want to present another option. What if this person already knows the end of the story? In fact, Jesus tells us how it all ends. In John 11 Jesus gets word that his friend Lazarus was sick. He waited a few more days to go see him, but by then Lazarus was dead. When Jesus came into the town of Bethany he was met by Martha, and the conversation they had revealed much about the end of the story. "Martha answered, 'I know he will rise again in the resurrection at the last day.' Jesus said to her, 'I am the resurrection and the life. The one who believes in me will live, even though they die'" (John 11:24–5 NIV).

Martha was confronted with the reality of her current situation and the knowledge of the kingdom. She was faced with the reality that her brother was dead, but she held on to the hope that one day her brother would rise again in the resurrection at the end of the day. Jesus added faith to the story when he said to her, "I am the resurrection and the life." These were profound words. As we all know at the end of this story Jesus raised Lazarus from the dead. Can you imagine the faith this act would have created in the heart of Martha? This man who just told her that He does not just possess resurrection power, He is resurrection power just raised her brother from the dead.

The reality of the human condition still rang true to Lazarus. Whether it was one year or twenty from that moment, Lazarus died. His earthly body could not live forever. But God, after his physical death, because of his new birth in Christ, resurrected him into eternity to live with Christ forever. This is the end of the story. This is what all the suspense is leading to. This is what we hope in, what we hope for; this is the power that we put our faith in. We put our faith and trust in the person who has defeated death because He does not possess resurrection power, He is resurrection power.

Paul writes a similar thing to the Church in Colossians, explaining why we can endure all hardship and speak the gospel without hesitation. He writes, "Because we know that the one who raised the Lord Jesus from the dead will also raise us with Jesus and present us with you to himself" (2 Corinthians 4:14 NIV).

At the end of the day, this life is not about me, and it's not about you. It is not about fulfilling my dreams or my being happy. God doesn't come into our story to give us a happy ending. Jesus buries our story at the foot of the cross and allows us to step into His story. The moment we step into His story the course of our lives changes. We no longer chase our dreams, we chase His. We no longer seek our own desires, we seek His. We no longer care what happens to us in this mortal life because we now have faith in the hope of the resurrecting power that is Jesus Christ, knowing that He will be faithful to His promise and though we may die, we will live.

ELEVEN

ETERNAL JUDGMENT

We cannot talk about the end of the story without talking about eternal Judgment. Oftentimes, when we think of judgment, we think of the word in a negative light. You constantly hear people say, "Don't judge me." Or, "Who are you to judge?" This is because when we put the word judgment in our mind, we instantly think of someone giving us a prison sentence, or someone making some sort of negative conclusion about us or the way we live life. But in truth everything positive or negative is a judgment. If I say you have a beautiful jacket, I made a judgment.

If we can take the negative context out of the word, we can begin to see the biblical context of eternal judgment. What we must understand about God is that He is holy. That is not just a characteristic of God; that is who He is. He is also just. *Just* is a word we try to understand, but we often confuse it with *fair*. The word *fair* denotes a win-win situation. We want to make sure there is even distribution. *Just* is similar, but it denotes a black-and-white result. It is based on truth. It does not care who wins; it simply finds the truth.

God is a just God. Sin cannot enter His presence. An Old Testament prophets says this of God. "Your eyes are too pure to look on evil; you cannot tolerate wrongdoing" (Habakkuk 1:13, NIV). He cannot look at sin without judgment, and He cannot pardon sin. This is why Jesus had to die. Jesus, being the perfect lamb who was sacrificed for our sin, was the only one who could fully erase our sin. All the sacrifices in the old covenant were inadequate to do this. At best they could merely appease the anger of a Holy God. When Jesus died, He traded places with us and became sin. He didn't just cover our sin; He erased it.

One day, at the end, when all is finished, the righteous will have been resurrected, and the devil will be in hell. Every soul that ever lived on the earth will come before God in what is called the white throne judgment (Revelation 20:11–15). This is where the Eternal God will sit and judge each one of us based on our deeds. This is bad news for all of us. But all of those who put their faith in Jesus, all those who answered His call because of the blood of Jesus will walk before the judge unashamed, without regret or condemnation can have confidence that when we stand before the Almighty, and when He looks at us, He will see Jesus's blood. He will say to us, "Well done, good and faithful servant! You have been faithful with a few things; I will put you in charge of many things. Come and share your master's happiness!"" (Matthew 25:23 NIV).

With this amazing hope, there is another side. When the Judge sitting on the throne opens the book of life—the book of those who are covered by the blood of Jesus—any person whose name is not found in that book will be cast into the lake of fire, where they will face eternal torture and death. This death is not physical death but spiritual, meaning complete separation from God.

This is how the story will end. What amazes me is that life on this earth is so short. It is so temporary. It is so fragile. And we waste it away every day chasing meaningless things that will not enter eternity. The enemy of God has put such glamor and shine on all the things of this world. And because of the fragile nature of life, we are tricked into believing that these temporary things should matter. But I want to tell you today, now that you know the end of the story, I pray that it opens your eyes and brings you to godly sorrow that leads to repentance. And right now, you will have a change of mind and will begin to think about godly things.

Paul says it like this: "Finally, brothers and sisters, whatever is true, whatever is noble, whatever is right, whatever is pure, whatever is lovely, whatever is admirable—if anything is excellent or praiseworthy—think about such things" (Philippians 4:8 NIV).

So what shall we do? Repent and be baptized. Once you have done that, find someone who is a model of godliness to you. Ask them to lead you and teach you the ways of the Bible. But don't just rely on them. Open the Bible for yourself. Read it as much as you can. When you sit down to read it, pray to God and ask Him to open your eyes and show you His truth. Let the Holy Spirit guide you in the lifelong process of learning and growing as we strive to be like Christ.

Don't be discouraged or lose heart. Remember what we have talked about and remind yourself daily that this life, this place is not my home. And long to be with Jesus every moment of your life. If you do this, the Holy Spirit will open your eyes to a new revelation. He will use you to do the miraculous. You will see God's glory shine through you as you point people to Him. And at the end of the day, I can promise you this. You will never look back on a life lived for Christ and feel like it wasn't worth the cost. In Him, we will find more love, acceptance, and value than you could ever find anywhere else in the world.

I hope this book spoke to your heart. And I have tried to explain these biblical truths to the best of my ability, and it is my prayer that where I am lacking the Holy Spirit will take over and continue to teach you until you reach the fullness of maturity in your walk with Him. I would like to encourage you not to take my word for it. But test it, judge it by the word of God. Let my words be judged by wise counsel, and always trust in Jesus and His word above mine. It is my goal to present biblical truth not from my opinion but through the revelation and illumination of His Word.

Lastly, I want you to always know that if you have this book, I am praying for you. I may not know you; I may not have any idea what is going on in your life. But I am praying for you. I pray first that God will give you a fresh revelation of who He is, that you will be able to hear Him and see Him in ways that you never imagined. Second, I pray that God will give you regeneration in your spirit. That God will make your soul prosper. That you will not grow weary from doing good. Third, I pray that you will have health in your body and strength in your body so you can complete the work that He has called you to do.

I call you blessed. May the grace of God rest on you all the days of your life. Amen.

Printed in the United States
by Baker & Taylor Publisher Services